LORRAINE HANSBERRY

POWER OF THE PEN

BLACK WOMEN WRITERS

by Joyce Markovics

NORWOOD HOUSE PRESS

For more information about Norwood House Press, please visit our website at:
www.norwoodhousepress.com or call 866-565-2900.

Book Designer: Ed Morgan
Editorial and Production: Bowerbird Books

Photo Credits: © Everett Collection/Newscom, cover and title page; © Everett Collection/Newscom, 5; Public Domain, 6; Wikimedia Commons, 7; Photo courtesy of the Lorraine Hansberry Literary Trust, LHLT.org, 8; The University of Chicago Public Library, 9; Library of Congress, 10; Schomburg Center for Research in Black Culture, Photographs and Prints Division, The New York Public Library, 11; Wikimedia Commons, 12; Schomburg Center for Research in Black Culture, Photographs and Prints Division, The New York Public Library, 13; Wikimedia Commons, 14; Photo courtesy of the Lorraine Hansberry Literary Trust, LHLT.org, 15; Schomburg Center for Research in Black Culture, Photographs and Prints Division, The New York Public Library, 16; Wikimedia Commons/Photographer-Friedman-Abeles, New York, 17; Wikimedia Commons/Felix Stahlberg, 18; © Joyce Markovics, 19; Wikimedia Commons/Nationaaal Archief, 20; © Glasshouse Images/Newscom, 21.

Hardcover ISBN: 978-1-68450-668-2
Paperback ISBN: 978-1-68404-977-6

Library of Congress Cataloging-in-Publication Data

Names: Markovics, Joyce L., author.
Title: Lorraine Hansberry / by Joyce Markovics.
Description: [Buffalo] : Norwood House Press, 2024. | Series: Power of the
    pen : Black women writers | Includes bibliographical references and
    index. | Audience: Grades 4-6
Identifiers: LCCN 2023045975 (print) | LCCN 2023045976 (ebook) | ISBN
    9781684506682 (hardcover) | ISBN 9781684049776 (paperback) | ISBN
    9781684049837 (ebook)
Subjects: LCSH: Hansberry, Lorraine, 1930-1965--Juvenile literature. |
    Women dramatists, American--Biography--Juvenile literature. | African
    American dramatists--Biography--Juvenile literature. | African American
    women dramatists--Biography--Juvenile literature. | LCGFT: Biographies.
Classification: LCC PS3515.A515 Z76 2024 (print) | LCC PS3515.A515
    (ebook) | DDC 812/.54 [B]--dc23/eng/20231002
LC record available at https://lccn.loc.gov/2023045975
LC ebook record available at https://lccn.loc.gov/2023045976

372N--012024

Manufactured in the United States of America in North Mankato, Minnesota.

CONTENTS

INTRODUCING LORRAINE

Lorraine Hansberry was a playwright. And she was a brilliant mind. She believed that words could change the world. Lorraine was the first Black woman to have a play on Broadway. It was called *A Raisin in the Sun*. "Never before, in the entire history of the American theater, had so much of the truth of Black People's lives been seen on the stage," said the writer James Baldwin. He was right. Throughout her short life, Lorraine shattered barriers. She fought for **racial justice**. And her success opened doors for other Black artists.

ASK YOURSELF
HOW DO YOU THINK WORDS ARE POWERFUL?

This is a portrait of Lorraine Hansberry from the 1960s.

LORRAINE'S BEST-KNOWN WORK IS *A RAISIN IN THE SUN*. SHE ALSO WROTE OTHER PLAYS, STORIES, AND ESSAYS. SHE EVEN WROTE A SCREENPLAY FOR TV!

EARLY YEARS

"I was born May 19, 1930, the last of four children," said Lorraine Vivian Hansberry. She entered the world at Provident Hospital in Chicago. It was the first Black-owned hospital in the country. Lorraine's family was strong and proud. Lorraine's dad Carl was a successful businessman. He worked in real estate. He also founded Lake Street Bank. Nannie, Lorraine's mom, was a teacher.

Lorraine was very bright. But she wasn't a great student. This is one of her yearbook photos.

IMPORTANT BLACK LEADERS VISITED LORRAINE'S HOME. THESE PEOPLE INCLUDED **ACTIVIST** W.E.B. DU BOIS, POET LANGSTON HUGHES, AND MUSICIAN DUKE ELLINGTON.

Lorraine's parents were both activists. They stood up against **segregation** and inequality. Lorraine went to school on Chicago's South Side. The area was rough. "The kids beat me up," said Lorraine. "From that moment I became a **rebel**." When Lorraine was eight, her family moved. They chose an all-white neighborhood. Some laws kept Black families out of white neighborhoods. That didn't stop Carl and Nannie.

Chicago in the 1930s when Lorraine was a young girl

> ## All racism was rotten, white or Black.

When Lorraine and her family moved into their new home, a white mob showed up. Not long after, a brick crashed through their window. It almost struck Lorraine. The police came to the house. One officer said, "Some people throw a rock through your window and act like it was a bomb." Young Lorraine never forgot the angry faces she saw that day. Afterward, her mom stayed up all night to keep watch. She wanted to protect her family.

Lorraine as a young woman

The white neighbors tried to force the Hansberrys to move. But Carl and Nannie fought back. They went to court—and won. Over time, the neighborhood began to change. More Black families moved there. However, that didn't stop the racist attacks. Lorraine recalls being spat on by white neighbors on her way to school.

Lorraine's family home (center) is now a Chicago landmark.

ASK YOURSELF
CAN YOU REMEMBER A HARD TIME IN YOUR LIFE? HOW DID IT MAKE YOU FEEL?

> **So many truths seem to be rushing at me as the result of things felt and seen and lived through.**

Lorraine attended Englewood High School. There, she became interested in theater. When the school tried to bring in more Black kids, the white students led a **strike**. Lorraine was frustrated. She wondered why more people didn't stand up for the Black students. She would later write about the event in her story "The Riot."

Racist signs like this appeared in Chicago and many other parts of the country.

When Lorraine was still in high school, **tragedy** struck. Her father suddenly died at age 50. She was only 15. The loss deeply affected her. "The man that I remember was an educated soul," said Lorraine after his death. "He carried his head in such a way that I was quite certain that there was nothing he was afraid of." In 1948, Lorraine graduated from high school. She set her sights on college.

Carl Augustus Hansberry, Lorraine's father

BEFORE HE DIED, LORRAINE'S FATHER HAD PLANNED TO MOVE HIS FAMILY TO MEXICO. HE THOUGHT THEY COULD LIVE MORE FREELY AND WITHOUT RACISM THERE.

HER WORK

> Write if you will: but write about the world as it is and as you think it ought to be and must be.

Lorraine went to the University of Wisconsin. She was the first Black woman to live in her **dorm**. In her first year, she sneaked into a theater. A play was being **rehearsed**. It was *Juno and the Paycock*. The play is about grief. It follows a mother whose son is murdered. Lorraine was **spellbound**. She was reminded of the violence she saw in Chicago. That day would change her life.

Juno and the Paycock is a work by the Irish playwright Seán O'Casey. "Paycock" is the Irish way of saying the word *peacock*.

12

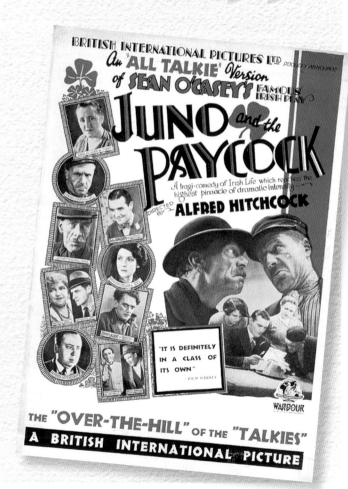

BRITISH INTERNATIONAL PICTURES LTD PRODUCTION ANNOUNCE

An "ALL TALKIE" Version of SEAN O'CASEY'S FAMOUS IRISH PLAY

JUNO and the PAYCOCK

A tragi-comedy of Irish Life which reaches the highest pinnacle of dramatic intensity

DIRECTED BY ALFRED HITCHCOCK

"IT IS DEFINITELY IN A CLASS OF ITS OWN" — FILM WEEKLY

WARDOUR

THE "OVER-THE-HILL" OF THE "TALKIES"
A BRITISH INTERNATIONAL PICTURE

In college, Lorraine also became more interested in **politics** and **civil rights** causes. She spoke out for many things. A classmate once said that Lorraine was "the only girl I knew who could whip together a fresh **picket sign** with her own hands, at a moment's notice, for any cause or occasion."

ASK YOURSELF
HAVE YOU EVER STOOD UP FOR SOMETHING YOU FELT STRONGLY ABOUT?

A portrait of Lorraine in the 1950s

> One cannot live with sighted eyes and feeling heart and not know or react to the miseries which afflict this world.

Lorraine left college before getting her degree. She quit "to pursue," as she said, "an education of another kind." She studied painting for a while. And then Lorraine moved to Harlem, New York. By 1951, she started writing for *Freedom*. The newspaper was founded by Paul Robeson, an actor and activist. The newspaper **advocated** for civil rights and world peace. It also took a strong stand against **white supremacy**.

The front page of the newspaper *Freedom*

Lorraine and Robert as a young couple. They separated in 1957 but remained good friends.

While working for *Freedom*, Lorraine traveled around the world. She wrote about civil rights issues abroad. A couple of years later, Lorraine met Robert Nemiroff. He was a Jewish writer. Robert shared many of Lorraine's views. In 1953, the couple married. In 1956, Lorraine quit the newspaper to write full-time. She started working on a play. It was called *A Raisin in the Sun*.

LORRAINE **IDENTIFIED** AS A **LESBIAN**. HOWEVER, IN THE 1950s, **HOMOSEXUALITY** WAS ILLEGAL IN NEW YORK CITY.

In her early twenties, Lorraine had written several plays. But she wasn't happy with any of them. *A Raisin in the Sun* felt different. Lorraine was inspired by her childhood in Chicago. She based the characters on people she knew. The play she wrote is about a Chicago family, the Youngers. At the start of the play, the family is about to receive a lot of money. And they must decide how to spend it. The outcome of their decision unifies the Youngers.

Many experts think *A Raisin in the Sun* is one of the best plays ever written. This is Lorraine in 1959 after finishing her play.

In 1959, the play **premiered** on Broadway. It was a huge hit. Famous actor and activist Sidney Poitier was in the **cast**. He said Lorraine was "reaching the **essence**" of who Black people "were, who we are, and where we came from." The play won the New York Drama Critics' Circle Award in 1959. Lorraine was the youngest person and first Black playwright to earn the award!

This is a scene from *A Raisin in the Sun*. The play was made into a movie in 1961.

LORRAINE FIRST CALLED HER PLAY *THE CRYSTAL STAIR*. THEN SHE CHANGED THE TITLE TO *A RAISIN IN THE SUN*. THAT NAME COMES FROM A LANGSTON HUGHES POEM. IN IT, HE ASKS, "WHAT HAPPENS TO A DREAM **DEFERRED**?/DOES IT DRY UP/LIKE A RAISIN IN THE SUN?"

> **The writing urge is on . . . only death or infirmity can stop me now.**

After the success of her first play, Lorraine wrote another. The title was *The Sign in Sidney Brunstein's Window*. Then, in 1963, Lorraine collapsed in pain. She was rushed to the hospital. There, doctors **diagnosed** her with cancer. Soon after, Lorraine picked up her pen and kept writing. Nothing could stop her.

The Sign in Sidney Brunstein's Window takes place in Greenwich Village in New York City. That's where Lorraine and Robert lived when they were married.

Lorraine's second play opened. And it ran for 101 performances. She wrote, "When I get my health back I shall go into the South." Lorraine worried that she wasn't doing enough to fight for civil rights. On January 12, 1965, *The Sign in Sidney Brunstein's Window* closed. That same day, Lorraine died. She was only 34 years old. Seven hundred people came to her funeral. Martin Luther King, Jr. said that Lorraine would "remain an inspiration to generations yet unborn."

Later in her life, Lorraine moved to Croton-on-Hudson, New York. The text on her gravestone is from *The Sign in Sidney Brustein's Window*. Part of it reads, "I care. I care about it all. It takes too much energy not to care."

ASK YOURSELF
HAVE YOU EVER LOST A LOVED ONE? WHAT WAS THAT LIKE?

IN 1970, *LES BLANCS*, ANOTHER PLAY BY LORRAINE, PREMIERED. ROBERT HELPED COMPLETE THAT PLAY AND MANY OF LORRAINE'S OTHER WORKS.

LORRAINE'S POWER

Through her plays, Lorraine changed the way Black people's lives were shown on stage. She made the theater a place where Black artists could freely express themselves. Even when she was ill, Lorraine never stopped creating. And she never stopped fighting for equality and justice.

Nina Simone was a singer, songwriter, and civil rights activist.

THE TALENTED SINGER NINA SIMONE TURNED LORRAINE'S WORDS INTO A SONG. SHE SANG, "YOUNG, GIFTED AND BLACK. OH WHAT A LOVELY PRECIOUS DREAM."

Before she died, Lorraine spoke to Black teens who had won a writing competition. She said, "Write about the world as it is and as you think it ought to be and must be . . . write about our people." In her soul, Lorraine believed in the power and beauty of Black people. "I think that the human race does command its own destiny," said Lorraine. "And that destiny can eventually embrace the stars."

ASK YOURSELF
LEGACY IS THE LONG-LASTING IMPACT OF A PERSON'S LIFE. WHAT KIND OF LEGACY WOULD YOU WANT TO LEAVE BEHIND?

Lorraine was one of the first people to proudly use the term *Black*.

TIMELINE AND ACTIVITY

May 19, 1930
Lorraine is born in Chicago, Illinois

1945
Lorraine's dad Carl dies

1948
Lorraine enrolls at the University of Wisconsin

1950
Lorraine leaves college

1959
A Raisin in the Sun premiers; Lorraine wins the New York Drama Critics' Circle Award

1964
Lorraine's second play, *The Sign in Sidney Brustein's Window*, premiers

January 12, 1965
Lorraine dies of cancer at age 34

GET WRITING!

Lorraine Hansberry is best known for being a playwright. Write a short play. Start with an outline of the story. What's the beginning, middle, and end? Decide on the characters. Now write a draft of your play. Share your work with an adult or friend!

GLOSSARY

activist (AK-tuh-vist): a person who fights for a cause.

advocated (AD-vuh-keyt-id): supported something.

cast (KAST): performers in a play.

civil rights (SIV-uhl RITES): the rights everyone should have to freedom and equal treatment under the law, regardless of who they are.

deferred (di-FURD): delayed or put off.

diagnosed (dye-uhg-NOHSD): identified what disease or illness a patient has.

dorm (DORM): a room where people sleep and live on a college campus.

essence (ES-uhns): the true nature or quality of something.

homosexuality (hoh-muh-sek-shoo-AL-ih-tee): being attracted to people of one's own sex or gender.

identified (ahy-DEN-tuh-fyed): indicated what something is.

justice (JUHS-tis): the quality of being fair and good.

lesbian (LEZ-bee-uhn): a woman who is attracted to other women; a gay woman.

picket sign (PIK-it SAHYN): a sign with a pointed stake at the end.

politics (POL-ih-tiks): having to do with government or running for and holding public office.

premiered (pri-MEERD): gave the first performance of.

racial (REY-shuhl): relating to race or ethnicity.

rebel (REB-uhl): someone who fights against those in charge.

rehearsed (ri-HURSSD): practiced for a performance.

segregation (SEG-rih-gay-shuhn): when Black people are kept separate from white people.

spellbound (SPEL-bound): to fascinate.

strike (STRIKE): when people refuse to do something based on a disagreement of some kind.

tragedy (TRAJ-uh-dee): a sad and terrible event.

white supremacy (WAHYT suh-PREM-uh-see): the false belief that white people are somehow better than other people, especially Black and Jewish people.

FOR MORE INFORMATION

Books

Hughes, Langston. *Poetry for Young People*. New York, NY: Union Square Kids, 2021.
Read some of Langston Hughes's most influential poems.

O'Neill, Bill. *The Great Book of Black Heroes*. Sheridan, WY: LAK Publishing, 2021.
Explore the lives of 30 incredible Black people.

Websites

Britannica Kids: Lorraine Hansberry
(https://kids.britannica.com/kids/article/Lorraine-Hansberry/399965)
Learn about Lorraine Hansberry's life.

PBS LearningMedia: Lorraine Hansberry
(https://ny.pbslearningmedia.org/resource/fp19.lgbtq.hansberry/lorraine-hansberry/)
Listen to an exploration of Lorraine Hansberry's work and accomplishments.

INDEX

ABOUT THE AUTHOR

Joyce Markovics has written hundreds of children's books. She's passionate about celebrating the lives and accomplishments of women. Joyce would like to thank the Lorraine Hansberry Literary Trust.